Kabodian

LAND OF THE SPOTTED EAGLE

LAND OF THE

A PORTRAIT OF
THE RESERVATION SIOUX

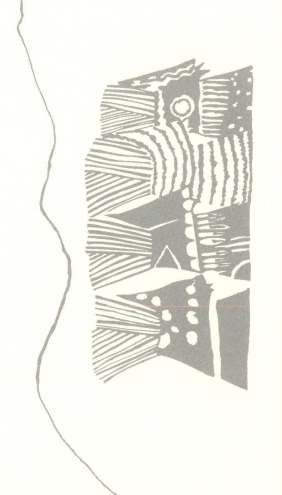

SPOTTED EAGLE

Harry W. Paige

Photographs by Don Doll, S.J.

LOYOLA UNIVERSITY PRESS
Chicago

LOYOLA UNIVERSITY PRESS
3441 North Ashland Avenue
Chicago, Illinois 60657

"Wounded Knee: The Tragedy and the Dream," "Epitaph for a Mixed Blood," and "Indian Space, Indian Time," reprinted from *The Westerners*, New York Posse Brand Book.

"The Vision of Noah Jumping Eagle," "Without Memories We Are As the Wind," "Mass Here, Mass There," and "If I Were the Last Christian" copyright 1972, 1982, 1973, and 1975 by the College of St. Thomas and reprinted by permission of *The Catholic Digest*.

"A Death on the Prairie" reprinted by permission of *America* magazine.

The illustrations on pages 7 and 71, are taken from the work of Amos Bad Heart Bull, an Oglala Sioux pictorial historian.

The drawings on pages 33, 43, and 65 are from the work of Kills Two, an Oglala Sioux artist.

Illustration on page 1 by permission of West Point Museum Collections, United States Military Academy

Library of Congress Cataloging in Publication Data

Paige, Harry W., 1922-
    Land of the spotted eagle.

    1. Oglala Sioux Tribe—Pictorial works.
2. Oglala Indians—Pictorial works. I. Title.
E99.03P35 1987   973'.0497   87-26252
ISBN 0-8294-0581-X

DESIGN, ILLUSTRATIONS FOR THE PAGE AND PART OPENING PAGES BY C.L. TORNATORE

Other books by Harry W. Paige:
Songs of the Teton Sioux
Wade's Place
Night at Red Mesa
Johnny Stands
The Summer War
Shadow on the Sun

Other books by Don Doll, S.J:
Crying for A Vision
"Hunters of the Bering Sea"
   in *National Geographic* magazine
Sioux Indian photographs
   in *A Day in the Life of America*

To the Lakota People

C O N T E N T S

P R E F A C E

I FIRST CAME TO THE LAKOTA IN THE EARLY 1960S LOOKING for knowledge, the knowledge of song, myth, and legend held mostly by the older people. This was on the Rosebud and Pine Ridge Reservations in South Dakota. After three summers I left with what I hoped was the beginning of wisdom, a wisdom into the things of the spirit, the things the older people call *wakaN*, the things that really matter in this life. I went to their Sun Dances, their Yuwipi Meetings, and I spent many hours talking with the older people about things *wakaN*.

Although there has been some material progress in the last twenty-five years or so, many of the chronic problems remain—unemployment, poverty, disease, alcohol abuse, government mismanagement, broken families, a confused and troubled youth. All these spectors remain along with the constant fear that the culture itself is dying.

The old people know, as do old people everywhere, that their individual lives will end before too many winters pass; but their greatest fear is that a way of life may be dying with them, a way of life which celebrates the special relationship they have with the land and its creatures, both four-leggeds and two-leggeds. And its special relationship with *WakaNtaNka*, the Great Spirit.

So while the younger people try to join the modern world and yet remain Indian, the old try to dream back the old days and the old ways. While the young and energetic have established the Sinte Gleska (Spotted Tail) College at Rosebud, the old dream their dreams. Sometimes, though, there isn't much to remember.

There isn't one person alive now who lived the old Plains culture that fired the imagination for a century before it died the long death of dreams. There isn't one now who has seen the buffalo running wild. Or seen the sacred *ptesaN*, the White Buffalo. Or a smoke signal. Or a scaffold burial. There isn't one warrior who has counted *coup* on an enemy—unless it be in one of the white man's long-range wars. Few have danced the Sun Dance when it

was a trial by courage, an ordeal suffered so that the people may live. Few have plucked the tail feathers from *WaNbli*, the Eagle, to wear proudly in the hair as a warrior's badge. Few have lived in tipis. Few young men have made the *HaNblecheyapi*, the Vision Seeking Quest, the test of manhood and the sacred rite by which a Lakota usually received his name. Few of the dying have sung their death songs—

Le wana henala! Now it is over!

What apology can one offer for being more than a century late?

Why a cultural post-mortem?

Why a portrait of the Reservation Sioux?

Because, if the Golden Age of the Sioux has fallen to the ground, the virtues that sustained it have not. There is courage now—not the quick, summoned courage of the warpath or the hunt but the courage of waiting, of hoping: the courage snatched from the jaws of despair. There is the courage to face tomorrow while remembering yesterday. And there is the courage to have faith, to believe in the things of the spirit and the dignity of man.

Because, in all their proud and colorful history the hardest time is now.

HARRY W. PAIGE
Clarkson University
Summer, 1987

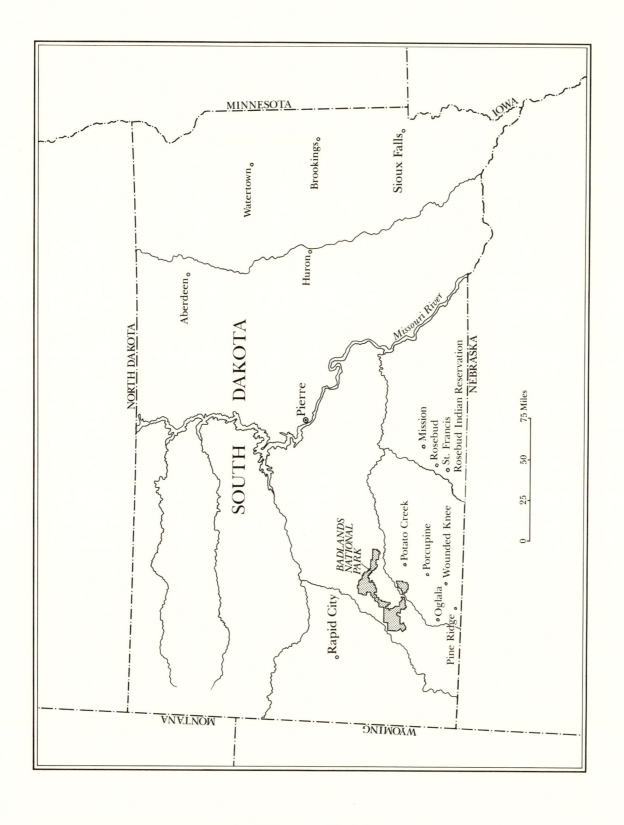

MINNESOTA

IOWA

Watertown

Brookings

Sioux Falls

Huron

Aberdeen

NORTH DAKOTA

SOUTH DAKOTA

Missouri River

Pierre

NEBRASKA

Mission

Rosebud

St. Francis

Rosebud Indian Reservation

75 Miles

50

Potato Creek

25

Porcupine

Wounded Knee

BADLANDS NATIONAL PARK

0

Rapid City

Oglala

Pine Ridge

MONTANA

WYOMING

A wedge of purple's passion on the map,
This martyr's worth of color separating browns;
A winter's cloud across the budding face of green,
Bead-scattered with the names of lonely towns:
Potato Creek, Calico, Oglala,
Pine Ridge and Wounded Knee—
Names that sift a story in their dust
And snatch the precious past from history.

All maps spread the geometric lie:
That what is drawn exact is also true—
With pastels that mark the symmetry of loss
And paint a purple legend of the Sioux.

THE TRAGEDY AND THE DREAM

THERE IS SOMETHING UNREAL about tragic places revisited. Gettysburg. Flanders. Omaha Beach. They challenge the historical imagination. They are always too peaceful. The sun is too bright. The sky cloudless perhaps and too painfully blue. The waves or sands or grass too meticulously constant in covering up the evidence. There is a postcard quality about such places. There is also something mildly conspiratorial about Nature's attempts to deny man's fragile grip on Time through memory.

Such a place is *Chankpe Opi*, Wounded Knee. It is a gentle place as prairie places go. The terrain rolls easily, unfolding the summer-burnished prairie grass cut only by the casual meanderings of Wounded Knee Creek. It is the sort of place that travel-weary tourists might choose for a roadside picnic. There is the hill where the four Hotchkiss guns once stood. There is the low flat beneath where Sitanka's ragged band of Minniconjou camped, restless in the shadow of the Blue Coats and their wagon guns. And there is the awful distance in between…

It happened at the height of the Ghost Dance trouble. Sitanka and his band of some three hundred men, women and children left their camp on the Cheyenne River just north of the mouth of Cherry Creek and started out for a council with Oglala Chief Red Cloud at Pine Ridge. Sitanka himself had a heavy chest cold that was to develop into pneumonia on the journey. But he thought it urgent to leave the Cheyenne River Agency and the nervous ring of soldiers that surrounded them, intent on stopping the Ghost Dancers from what the whites thought was a war dance. The ailing Chief wanted desperately to get to Red Cloud and what he thought of as the security of Pine Ridge, one hundred miles away.

The winter flight was a hard one. The band had to hunt along the way and game was scarce. The women and children slowed them down. The weather was against them. Sitanka was racked by fever; fits of coughing shook his thin frame like a dance rattle.

On the last leg of the journey, about halfway between Porcupine and Wounded Knee, near the pine-covered breast of Porcupine Butte, they were intercepted by a contingent of the U.S. Seventh Cavalry with Major Whiteside in command. The Seventh was Custer's old outfit. The memory of the Little Big Horn was only fourteen years old.

The Indians were surprised and alarmed. They flew the white flag of truce and waited. The afternoon of the twenty-eighth of December was a long one.

Immediately upon contact with the Indians the soldiers had formed battle lines, with machine guns drawn in place. Then the Indians were ordered to proceed to the Army camp at Wounded Knee Creek. They were told that later they would be allowed to go on to their destination, the Agency at Pine Ridge.

When General Brooke heard of the capture he sent Colonel George A. Forsyth, Commander of the Seventh, with reinforcements to guard the Indians. The Army had a total of 470 men and the battery of Hotchkiss guns. Less than one third of the three hundred Sioux were warriors.

The morning of December twenty-ninth broke bright and cold. The bugle sounded reveille; the echo hung frosty-clear in the valley of Wounded Knee before it shivered to silence. Colonel Forsyth ordered his men to disarm the Indians whose tipis had been set up on a flat just west of the Creek.

At about eight o'clock the warriors left their lodges to permit the search. The soldiers began tearing up the insides of the lodges in their hunt for anything that might be used as a weapon. They confiscated not only a small number of guns but knives, tools, bone awls and other things as well, and, survivors testified, they showed no regard for the privacy of the women and treated them roughly.

Medicine man Yellow Bird went about among the Indians blowing on an eagle-bone whistle, exhorting them to resist, assuring them that their Ghost Shirts made them invulnerable to the bullets of the soldiers. So a shot rang out. A soldier crumpled and fell. The valley of Wounded Knee exploded in confusion and death.

Within minutes, two hundred Indians and sixty soldiers lay dead or dying. The Indian survivors fled in wild panic toward the relative safety of the north-running dry ravine. The soldiers became a mob: discipline dissolved in confusion and rage. They chased the Indians, cutting them down as they fled: Women, children, old people, the wounded. Bodies were found later as far as two miles from where the first shots were fired.

When it was over, the soldiers left with the wounded and headed for Pine Ridge. Later, in the terrible quiet that came with dark the sky turned angry, the winds turned around and it began to snow. As though to cover up what had happened, the winter shroud draped itself mercifully over the scene.

On New Year's Day, 1891, a volunteer civilian burial party, escorted by soldiers to protect them, returned to the scene. Luckily, someone had the foresight to send medical supplies in case someone had survived. From a distance it seemed that the blizzard had softened the shape of the carnage. But up close it was not so. Most of the bodies were frozen in the strict geometry of violent death.

Miraculously, a few were still alive: a baby trying to nurse from its dead mother's breast; an old man clutching the splinters of his legs; a young girl hugging the bloody bank of the dry ravine as though it were a lover.

After the looting and the stripping of the Ghost Shirts from the dead bodies, after the picture taking, the bodies were piled up like cordwood, then dumped into the common grave. There were some tears from among the Indians in the burial party. A few death songs were sung. But that was all that redeemed the moment....no ceremonies, either Christian or native.

Today, a Catholic chapel shadows the hilltop. Its pale consecration seems right, as though it had risen in spiritual protest. Behind is the cemetery, dominated by the mass grave, eighty feet long and bordered in cement. There are other more recent graves but they are no more than mild rises or depressions in the earth, marked by crosses or small granite blocks and strewn with plastic flowers, even sadder because they refuse to wilt.

On a few graves there are indigenous, colored stones no bigger than a fist. Their meaning is *wakaN*—holy, mysterious. There is something about their scattering that makes most people leave them alone. Perhaps because they are too much like crystalized tears.

Some say that the mass grave covers the bones of nearly 150 men, women and children. The bodies of the rest were removed from the frozen field by friends and relatives for secret burial. Others died later in hastily improvised hospitals at the Agency in Pine Ridge, seventeen miles away.

The concrete curbing around the graves seems redundant, even ostentatious. It is a city effect, this neat and tidy border to death. It is not the prairie way. The prairie seems to have no patience with cement. The two are natural enemies. Even now the ants are at work—finishing what winter ground swells had started.

Adjacent to the trench is a nine foot, weathered monument on a concrete base. The south side of the death-gray marker tells:

This monument is erected by surviving relatives and other Ogallala and Cheyenne River Sioux Indians in Memory of the Chief Big Foot Massacre Dec. 29, 1890.

Col. Forsyth in command of U.S. Troops. Big Foot was a great chief of the Sioux Indians. He often said "I will stand in peace till my last day comes." He did many good and brave deeds for the white man and the red man. Many innocent women and children who knew no wrong died here.

June 18, 1930, the erecting of this monument is largely due to the financial assistance of Joseph Horn Cloud whose father was killed here.

The grammar, the syntax is not that of English professors but of people who still hurt. It is a writing that weeps.

A winter sorrow is not a summer sorrow. December on the prairie is often a gray and frozen time when the sun smolders through thin clouds and the sky threatens snow. The prairie wind wears a winter edge and screams to try its sharpness on fence, cattle or human. Little swirls of snow drift around aimlessly, sweeping delicate piles to rest in the corners of things. In summer, indeterminate grays sharpen and brighten to pastels. The wind still blows, but it blows warm, stirring up life instead of cold-whispering to death. Summer tries to make light of sorrow, hiding it in the shadows. Summer is for now, discouraging memory.

You think about a mother and her child running for the cover of the dry ravine as the bullets ricochet and splatter into the hard ground around her. She runs a frantic zig-zag course, drawing up her trailing buckskins with one hand and clutching the wrapped baby with the other. You imagine a soldier on horseback chasing her—hooves ringing—sword cutting figures in the air, loud now with screams and curses. Then, as he draws alongside—

Something intrudes. Some sound perhaps. The backfire of a pickup truck with its singing load of Indian children on the way to the Trading Post. The shrill, nervous chatter of a lonely bird. Or the intrusion may be visual: a hawk in floating crucifixion against the sky. Then you wake to summer as to a dream, leaving the Indian woman and her baby still running somewhere in a distant winter nightmare....

It is hard to imagine that something ended here in this peaceful valley. Endings should be *crescendo*. Proclaimed from the mountain top. In a voice of Thunder. Or written large in flame. It would be far easier to imagine that something *began* here. A seedling. A love. Or a prayer. It is an unlikely place for an ending—as unlikely as Appomatox. Yet that is what the footnote says: *the*

shooting between the races ended here. The long and bloody Indian Wars ended here "...not with a bang" as the poet says, "but a whimper"—the whimper of a child beneath a bloody blanket in the snow.

Today, there is talk of a Wounded Knee Memorial to be erected by an association of white men. They have already purchased a large chunk of land near the mass grave site. Part of this includes the dry ravine where so many Indians died while trying to escape. The memorial, complete with an "eternal flame," will be surrounded by a motel, Trading Post and other concessions for the tourists.

Many of the Indians are concerned about selling the bones of their dead. Many are questioning the motives of those who would make symbolic amends while also making hard cash. The arguments for the project are all too familiar ones: more Indian jobs, more tourists, more money.

If the project is realized it could be a second tragedy at Wounded Knee. The place is already *makoce wakaN, hallowed ground.* The plain monument is porous and chipped but it is *right*: it is a poor man's monument, an Indian monument. The words were written with a good heart. And they are true words. The monument stands like an eroded dream after the passing of the fact.

A dream. That was how Black Elk remembered Wounded Knee from the high hill of his old age:

And I can see that something else died there in the bloody mud, and was buried in the blizzard. A people's dream died there. It was a beautiful dream.

But Black Elk's sad verdict was premature. It didn't die there. Dreams die hard on the prairie. It doesn't matter much that tears are their only water and memory their only shade. Prairie dreams don't need much more. Just a people to keep them and a place to keep them in. A people like the Sioux. A place like Wounded Knee.

Author's note: Since the writing of this article, Wounded Knee has once again been the scene of conflict and bloodshed between Indians and whites as well as a symbol of the oppression as it exists on Pine Ridge.

On February 27, 1973 several hundred armed Indians captured the tiny community to dramatize their plight, bringing world-wide attention to the tragic place once again.

E P I T A P H

FOR A MIXED BLOOD

CALL HIM ROY. He was born in the winter of 1899, missing the new century by just a few months—a circumstance that seemed to set a pattern for his life. A pattern of too early, too late or in between.

He was born nine years after the infamous massacre at Wounded Knee, the last military engagement between Indians and whites and the bloody climax to the so-called Indian Wars. By 1899 the old, free life was dead and buried and the strange, new, wasting life in twentieth century America hadn't quite begun. So Roy was born in a cultural limbo, at a time when the Indian was still drifting in yesterday's wake, within sight of neither shore.

Roy was born in Mission, South Dakota—a sunbaked, wind-raked, near-treeless prairie crossroads where nothing much happened but time and the weather. Physically, the town is located in the heart of the Rosebud Sioux Reservation but its status is vaguely defined: usually it is considered an independent town. The largest community on the Reservation, it is the one place where Indians can buy liquor legally and drink at the white-owned bars that stab their neon arrows at the Indians' thirst. So Roy's birthplace was a neither-here-nor-there kind of a place, a physical and emotional no-man's land between prairie horizons.

Roy's father was French and his mother a full-blooded Sioux. And because his father was a traveling man, Roy was raised by his mother and his maternal grandmother. His father disapproved, but not enough to give up his traveling and settle down on the Reservation. He forbade the boy to speak Indian, but while he was away young Roy learned Lakota and spoke it, especially with *UNci*, his grandmother, who knew little English.

From the old woman with the dark, leathery, spiderwebby face he learned not only the language but also the myths and legends of the Sioux. All his life he

7

could remember his grandmother's stories about *Iktomi*, the Spider-Trickster and her stories about how the rabbit lost its tail and why the mudhen has red eyes and how the rainbow came to be. He thought they were beautiful stories—stories that seemed to drop from the purse of the old woman's mouth lyric as gently falling water. He could remember too the keening of the lullabies—the long, drawn-out syllables and then the soft explosion of words: *inila! Be still! istiN'ma yo!* Go to sleep!

His father sold Indian handicrafts and art work, buying them for next to nothing from the impoverished, sometimes desperate Indians and selling them to curio shops and tourist traps at inflated prices. Sometimes Roy went with him on his selling trips to Rapid City, Sioux Falls, or even Denver and Chicago. And then he would find himself in the strange, harsh world of the whites, where a man seemed to be measured by his money and the influence and the loudness of his voice. A world of all-night card games and the stench of whisky and the painted smiles of grub-pale women who rang with jewelry and looked like they were made of dough.

And during these times Roy didn't know if he was an Indian trying to be white or a white man trying to be Indian. So for most of his early years he wandered lost and lonely in the drafty chambers of his own heart.

Roy remained an only child, missing the warm, secure kinship ties that most of his acquaintances enjoyed. His father's trips back to the Reservation became less frequent and finally stopped altogether. Then there was a letter explaining that he had settled permanently in Chicago. After that, a few letters a year bore that postmark, letters that sometimes contained several carefully folded five dollar bills for the boy. By the time he was ten his father was no more than a memory and Roy lived out his aborted childhood under the protective warmth of maternal wings. From time to time an ill-defined feeling came over him—a feeling like regret, and he found himself missing the loud, assertive, confidence of the masculine perspective. Particularly when he went to a rodeo or an Indian celebration or a Sun Dance.

Roy spent most of his time searching for his childhood, even while it was running through his fingers like sunlight. He never found it. He always remained an outsider looking in. When he played cowboys and Indians, he was fair game for either side. In Valentine, Nebraska, he was treated as an Indian. In the full blood community of St. Francis, South Dakota, twenty-five miles southwest of his home, he was treated as white. If, at a summer picnic, there was free watermelon for Indians—he was white. At a white picnic—he was Indian. He seemed always to be standing on the cruel, barbed perimeter of life. And from any point on its circumference Roy stood apart and watched, hungry or lonely or scared.

For years he had a recurring dream inspired by an old priest's quotation from the Old Testament: *And King Solomon said, Divide the living child in two, and give half to the one, and half to the other.* He would wake from his restless sleep in terror, having seen the sword hanging over him. Then he would cry out for his grandmother who would come on swift and silent feet to sweep the sword away, sitting in the shadow of his fear until he fell asleep again.

The full bloods called Roy *ieska*, the Lakota word for *mixed blood*, meaning "he talks white." It was an expression that went back to the days of the fighting between Indians and whites, back to the belief among the Indians that those of mixed ancestry had sold them out,

Roy *did* talk white. But he talked Indian too. He was proud of the fact that he could talk for hours and not use a single *WasicuN*, English, word. He spoke as near a pure Lakota as you were likely to find. Even the older "long hairs" admitted, though somewhat grudgingly, that Roy talked "pretty good Indian." The harsh gutturals rattled in his throat and came out soft as a German lullaby. His nasals hummed like the wind in prairie wire. He could make the language flow, so that even if you didn't understand the words you got the idea that something wise or beautiful was being said.

In his childhod, Roy was beautiful. In his youth, he was handsome. In his older years he looked distinguished, even in his faded jeans and denim work shirt. He had a full head of dark brown hair that turned gray and then white with the slow, almost imperceptible grace of the seasons changing. His features were sharp, his cheek-bones high, forming a plateau beneath the striking blue-green eyes that looked out like turquoise set in a pale and predatory mask.

Roy quit school when he was sixteen to try to make a farm out of what had become his place—a brooding, tarpaper shack that seemed to squat like a dark bird hatching loneliness on ten acres of raw, Dakota prairie. But it was more like gardening than farming. They had ten head of cattle, some scrawny chickens and a garden

plot that was constantly under attack by hail, drought and grasshoppers.

One winter three head froze to death standing belly-deep in drifted snow so they looked like draped statues waiting to be unveiled. In summer an early July hailstorm pelted the garden into the ground, where it lay strewn and wilted like a thrown-out salad. The hailstones, big as golf balls, had rained sudden death on six of their chickens.

Roy fought a losing battle with the stubborn, flinty land until World War I came along. Then he surrendered his failing garden to the prairie and joined the Army, even though he wasn't an American citizen but a "ward" of the government. He said goodbye to his mother and his blind, old *UNci* who lived in a darker world of fleeting dreams crossed by wisps of memory. And then he left all he had known of life to become a warrior like his people before him.

He was assigned to an infantry unit and was considered, from the beginning, a good soldier. He took orders well and could give them too. He was a crack shot and he was popular with his fellow soldiers who accepted him as a white man with just enough Indian blood to be called Chief. But two weeks before his outfit was scheduled to sail for France, Roy broke his hip in training maneuvers and had to watch from his hospital bed as his company shipped out with the bands playing the tunes of glory over the strict cadence of marching feet. He had two operations on the hip and lay around for months until he came to hate the sharp, antiseptic smells and the starched, hovering nurses who stalked the midnight corridors like nervous, rustling birds.

One day as he lay staring from the window into the early, green explosion of a southern spring, he received a letter from his mother telling him that his grandmother had died. A single tear coursed down Roy's cheek, as though it was all he could spare for the memory of his lost childhood and his grandmother's passing. But that night in the echoing stillness of the place he thought of the old stories one by one until he finally fell asleep in the gentle swell of memory.

In time the doctors gave up on his hip and Roy was discharged, sent limping back to the Reservation with what he felt to be the shame of a non-combat wound. There he watched the return of warriors, heroes from across the big water—heroes celebrated by the Indian people in song, dance and Give-away ceremonies. Some came back strung with medals. Some with missing limbs, waving the sack of an arm at the honoring crowd. Some came back in plain, wooden boxes—native sons packaged for the dry Dakota earth. But no matter how they returned, Roy envied them. The living had a place to return to and the dead were forever of that place.

The decade of the 1920s was a disaster for most Reservation Indians. They had sold their cattle for high wartime prices and then had squandered the money. Their land was bought up or stolen by the rapidly growing number of whites on the Reservation. Tribal leadership fragmented and then collapsed. Malnutrition, alcoholism and other health problems increased. So did crime. Despair smoldered like a slow fuse in the hearts of the Indian people.

Roy did odd jobs around the Reservation and looked

after his failing mother. He walked with a telling limp but still managed to clerk in one of the Trading Posts, do some unskilled carpentry and some short-order cooking.

In 1924, the year the Indian was granted citizenship, Roy married a nineteen-year-old mixed-blood Cheyenne from a Nebraska border town. She ran a little restaurant her father had left her in the dusty, wind-swept community that seemed to have sprung like tough grass from the bleak Nebraska Sandhills. So Roy and his mother moved in the small apartment behind the restaurant, selling their old place and the land that went with it. When he signed over the deed to the new, white owner, Roy's fingers trembled on the pen and his heart knotted. A current of loss ran through him when he realized that he was signing away the Indian part of his life—his ties with the land and the mystical relationship that sprang from it. As he walked away from the signing the silver jingled in his pockets, but it sang a white man's song. A thin, metallic sound. Not like the surging heartbeat of the drums.

In contrast to the '20s, the '30s were good times. The Tribe had voted to incorporate so it could borrow money and start business enterprises. FDR's, Secretary of Interior Ickes and Commissioner of Indian Affairs John Collier made progress in raising the Indians' standard of living. Relief programs were instituted. The CCC had an Indian Division. There was the WPA and the Emergency Relief Administration. The U.S. Public Health Service set up hospitals and clinics to serve the needs of the Indian people. Cattle cooperatives were established. Dams, highways and other public projects were built.

Roy and his wife had three children in their first

seven years of marriage—two girls and a boy. He was a good father, following the Indian idea of letting the child develop in his own way, free from the pressures of the white world. He also encouraged them to discover their Indianness, but his encouragement was vague and divorced from example and so the children lived from day to day, blown about by the winds of caprice.

The name of the restaurant was changed from Emily's Place to Roy's Place, a concession to Roy's popularity with Reservation Indians and his knowlege of their language. Even an old Indian from some neglected corner of the prairie could come in Roy's Place and order in Lakota, saying *pejuta sapa* (black medicine) for *coffee* and *aguyapi* for *donuts*. Roy would figure out what they wanted and make them feel at home. The whites came to Roy's Place too—farmers, ranchers, cowhands and truck drivers. And for the first time in his life he began to think it was an advantage to be a mixed-blood Indian. Roy welcomed them all, kept the incessant kidding from touching raw nerves and acted as genial host as well as counterman.

Then, just as things seemed to be going well for Roy, his fortune turned around like an October wind and blew cold. His mother died suddenly, breathing her last from the depths of a peaceful sleep. A few weeks after his mother's funeral, Roy's young wife, worn gaunt by the prairie loneliness, drudgery and what she thought of as a boxed-in future, ran off with a truck driver from Omaha. Roy met these latest reversals with his characteristic attitude of resignation. He continued to run the place for a year and then sold it and moved back to Mission where he got a job as a clerk in a feed store.

Roy's life now centered around his children and his attempt to discover the half of him that was Indian. For the first time since the old days with his grandmother he consciously *tried* to be Indian. He went to *Yuwipi* meetings, held in tar-paper cabins on remote parts of the Reservation. He sat in the pitch blackness, a darkness exploding in drum beats and the wild cries of the singers, waiting for the spirits to appear. He asked the spirits, through the medium of a grizzled, old shaman, for faith in things Indian. For faith and the courage to believe.

Roy and his children went to the annual Sun Dance and watched as the votaries tried to rip their flesh loose from the thongs that bound them to the Sun Dance pole. He watched the dancers envious of their faith in the power of *Wi*, the Sun and *WakaNtaNka*, the Great Spirit. Envious even of their pain. And sometimes he would hear the echo of his inner prayer, beating to the heavy drums or the frantic rhythms of his own heart: *WakaNtaNka, uNshimala yo!* Great Spirit, have pity on me!

He tried to work himself up to a fever pitch of inner excitement, driven by the drum, the rattle, the bells, the screams of the eagle bone whistle and the passion to be a part of some remote blood-urge he couldn't quite understand. He tried, like his full-blooded friends to find magic in the commonplace. To find power in a stone or the tail feather of a hawk. He would finger a stone or a sunflower like a blind man touching his mother's face after a long absence. He would listen to the bird cries that came in the night, straining to catch the meaning that rose on a flurry of feathers. He packed his old jalopy and took his children to Custer State Park in the Black Hills to see the herds of buffalo—the buffalo that had once been the commissary-on-the-hoof for the Indian people. He tried to see it in all its power and sacredness and point out these mysteries to his children. But all he could see was a dumb beast, pawing the ground in fire-eyed, snorting meanness.

He went to some of the meetings of the Native American Church, the Peyote Cult, and ate peyote mash from a tarnished, ceremonial spoon. At first, he became sick at the stomach and later, when the visions came, they were terrifying: a vision of absolute whiteness, an arctic whiteness and then an icy fist closing on his heart or else the old, familiar nightmare of his childhood—the dividing sword suspended above his head.

Try as he might, Roy could not discover the blood truths of his Indian heritage. His curse was the white man's rational perspective that threw its light even into the darkest corners of the heart, exposing things for what they seemed to be in a naked, harsh glare.

With World War II came the end of the relative prosperity of the '30s. Times were harder than ever. And once again, Roy watched them march off to war. He was too old, too lame, and his son was too young. Another World War had passed him by like a big parade, leaving him to wrestle with feed sacks and fertilizer while half the world burned. For the people on the Reservation it was as though the war were thousands of light miles away. Their sons, who came back heroes or corpses, reminded them. And once, a heavy bomber, a B-17, crashed on the Reservation a few miles from where Roy lived. He was one of the first to reach the spot and help pull the broken bodies of the airmen from the wreckage.

The decades of the '50s and '60s were Roy's posthumous years. He watched his children grow up to inherit his own legacy of a quartered heart. He watched them grow up to obscurity and neglect, making the same mistakes he had made, searching the same ashes for the same distant clues.

In 1968 Roy decided to go out into the white man's world. A friend who ran a small grocery store in Denver invited him to work there. By this time Roy's children had all married whites and had left the Reservation for good. In Denver, living beneath the great stone shadow-wings of the Rockies, his heart ached for a prairie kind of loneliness, the empty miles that made every man anonymous. In the midst of a city crowd he would suddenly feel horribly alone and his heart would turn to cold marble. If he were condemned to be alone, Roy felt that he would rather be alone by himself in the great open spaces that shrunk the self to the size of a grain of prairie sand.

But Roy put off his return to the prairie until it was too late. He died in 1969 at the age of seventy, the victim of a sudden heart attack. He died a city death, dropping to the sidewalk like a stricken bird, spilling his life on dead concrete.

He missed the decade of the '70s by less than a year—but that didn't really matter. Time only seemed to increase the distance between Roy and the Self he was seeking.

His son who was living in Omaha at the time, claimed the body and had it returned to the Reservation. As there wasn't any plot available near his mother or his grandmother, Roy was buried between a full-blooded Indian and a white missionary priest. After paying the funeral expenses his son couldn't afford a headstone, so the church marked the grave with a piece of marble about the size of a brick. No words—not even his dates—were carved on it.

Roy's real epitaph was his life. An epitaph for a nomad heart. By itself, it was only the fraction of a life. Multiply it by thousands and you have a lonely caravan of shadows in search of substance. The old full blood in his isolated prairie shack knows that the old ways are over. He has watched them die. But he can summon up ancient ghosts at will, knowing that he has a home among them.

He has his blood ties with the land. He belongs. The white man too belongs—if not to what exists, then to what he has created. But the Roys, the mixed bloods, are the hostages of fortune.

Roy himself summed it up once over a cup of coffee and a cigarette. He tilted back his head and blew a smoke ring at the open window, watching until it stretched away to nothing. "You know," he said wearily, as though the words had suddenly floated to the surface of his mind, "being half anything is *waste sni*—no good."

And then, after a long pause, he said: "*Hecetu!*" It is so!

13

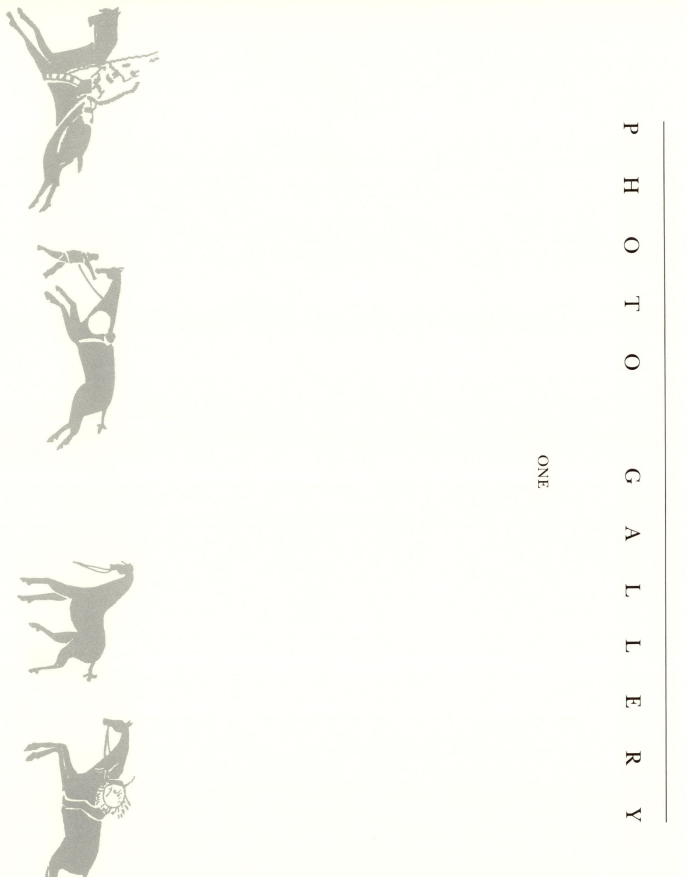

PHOTO GALLERY

ONE

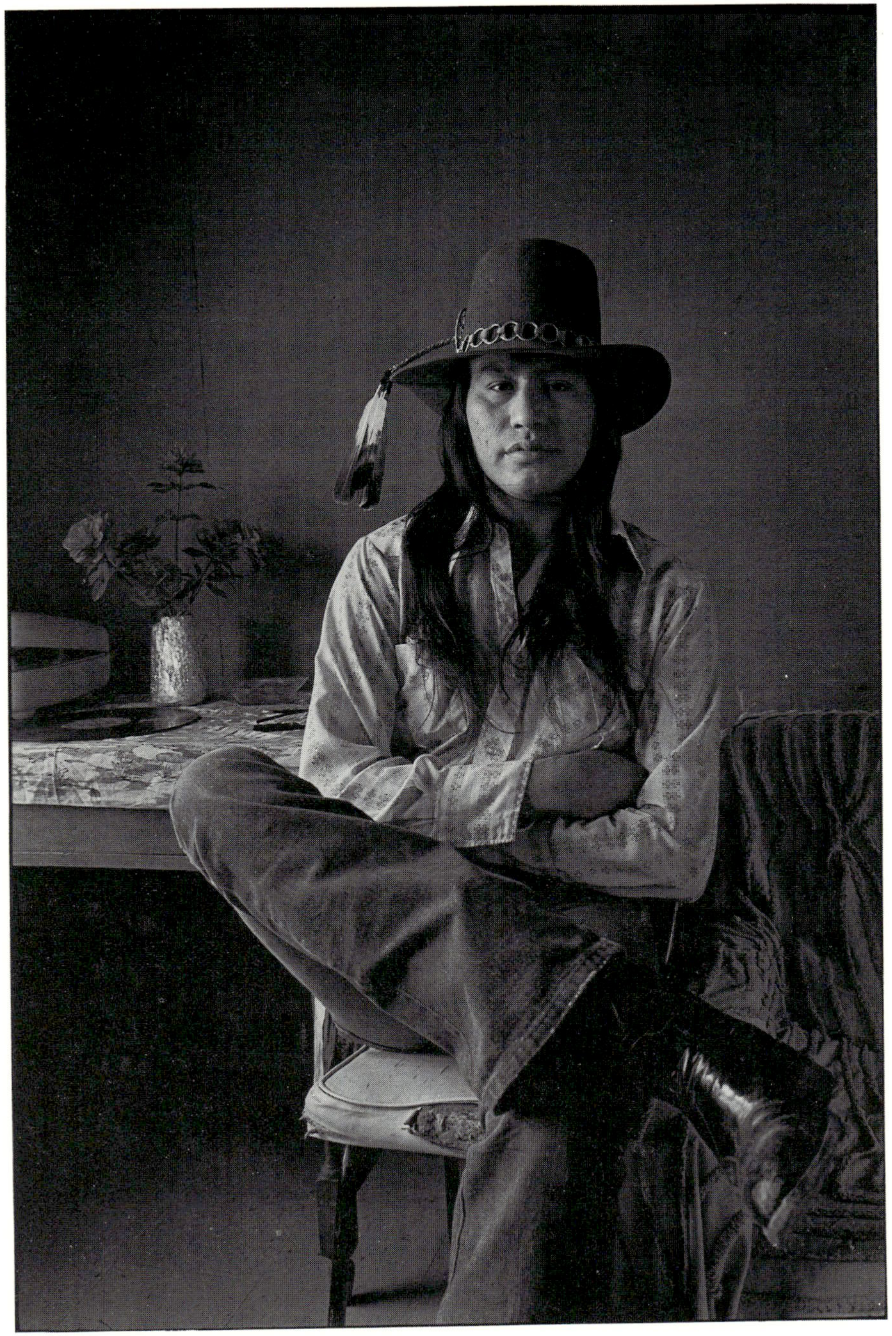

Sewel Makes Room for Them

Clouds east of Spring Creek

Charles Kills in Water on his 83rd birthday

Road to Spring Creek

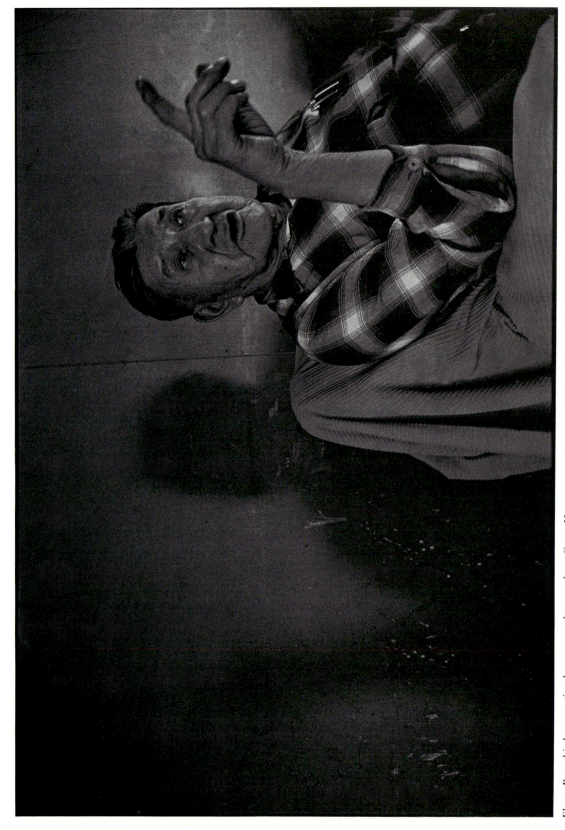

Elmer Bravebird recounting how no one knows where Crazy Horse is buried

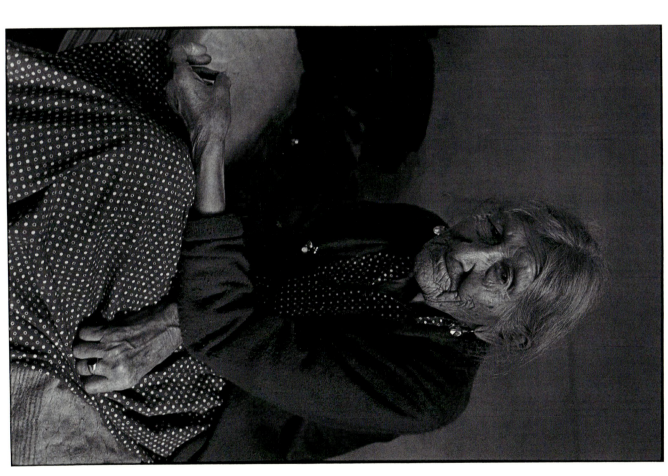

The Cloudman's stove and coffee pot

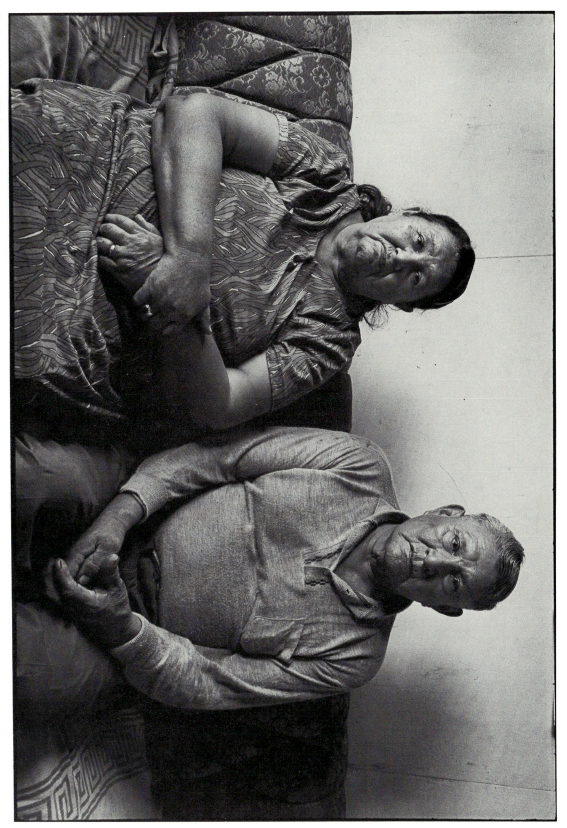

Ann Rose White Hat with Tyrone, Camille, Marlon and JJ

Lillian and Louie Walking Eagle with Cornell

Jack Menard and Linda Eagledeer's infant

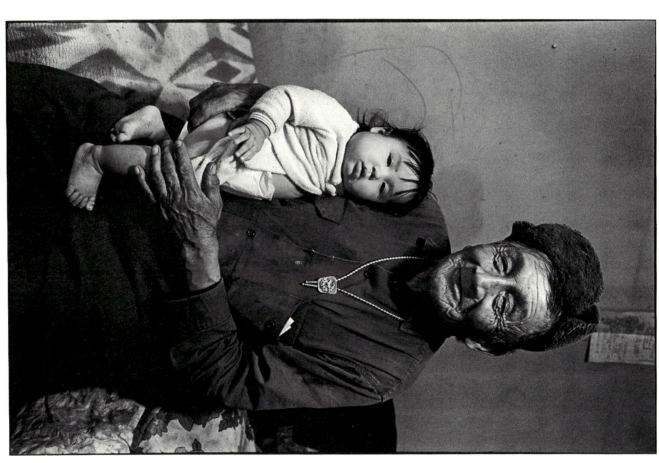

Leo Makes Room for Them with Rocky

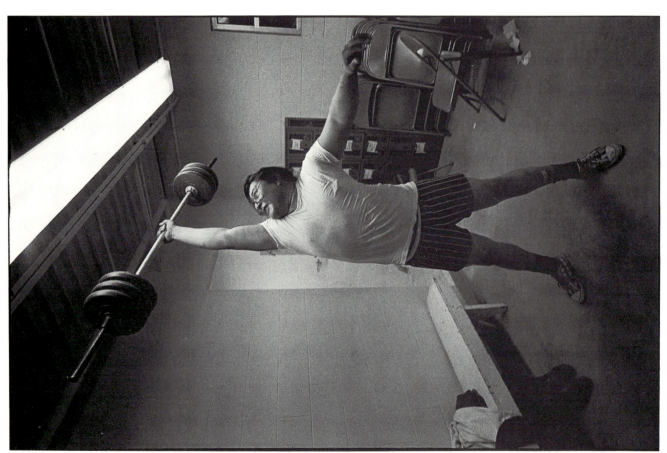

Morris Kills in Sight

Billy and Mervin Marshall round up their horses

Abraham Kills in Sight

INDIAN TIME

"TIME is but the stream I go a-fishing in. I drink at it; but while I drink I see the sandy bottom and detect how shallow it is. Its thin current slides away, but eternity remains."

—*Thoreau in Walden*

IT IS ALMOST IMPOSSIBLE TO WRITE OF THE SIOUX INDIAN country of South Dakota without resorting to hyperbole and cliche. There is the "big sky," sometimes painfully blue and crossed by billowing clouds that seem to stall on their own creativity, spinning themselves into something grander from within. There is the "timeless" easy sweep of the "sea of grass" rolling like an autumn-burnished tide toward some retreating shore. There is the sun that blazes with the first eye of creation. There is the imperceptible ghost-sculpturing of erosion, sharpening everything that rises high into a Gothic of needle points. There is the violence of mood and weather that breaks beneath the angry wings of what the Sioux call Thunder Beings…

But these
are physical
realities
and
belong
to space.
Time has no such reality—apart from the experience of time.

I hadn't been on the Rosebud Reservation in south-central South Dakota a week before I knew the difference between Indian-time and clock-time. Perhaps *knew* is the wrong word: it should be *felt*. For there, among the canyons and table-top buttes, time flows like a lazy river meandering toward some distant sea. It is a river that uncovers things—but slowly, sifting the sands along a gentle wash of miles, lapping at the shore with a curious rather than a hungry tongue. An arrowhead, porous and smaller than one might imagine and shaped for the hunt or the warpath is uncovered. A century falls away with no more splash than a small fish leaping at a fly. An ashen buffalo skull rolls into the water, its jagged, empty sockets upturned into a timeless, vacant stare. *TataNka.* The buffalo. Perhaps the sacred *ptesan*, the white buffalo. Now only a hollow god to join the fish and other floating things. Another century undercut and sucked into the swell of time.

From the past through the present to the future. From memory through now to anticipation. The succession seems cruelly irreversible though old men cling to yesterday and children reach for tomorrow.

But the river does not reverse itself. The buffalo skull with its weight of sand lies on the muddy bottom where fish explore the caverns of its sightlessness. The arrowhead sifts upstream in watery, capricious flight.

What man cannot understand he can always measure. Particularly if he has the quantitative European perspective that is his fragile revenge against the mysterious processes of nature through eternity. He fragments and dissects and by reducing the whole to the sum of its parts he believes he has accomplished something. No matter that the specimen frog is no longer a frog. No matter that all the scientists' horses and all the scientists' men couldn't put it together again.

The Sioux divided also but theirs were the logical divisions of natural man. They divided, but not to conquer. Winters, moons, sleeps—these were accurate enough: there was no need for hours, minutes, seconds, fractions of seconds. No need for epochs, eons, centuries. For the natives, *things* happened, not *time.* The Sioux

calendars, which they call Winter Counts, are pictograph drawings of *events.* Not ledgers of abstract numbers that refer to nothing in reality…or too much.

Thus 1881 was "the Winter that Spotted Tail Died" and 1890, "the Winter that Big Foot Was Killed!" (Wounded Knee Massacre). Logically, 1900 was "the Winter That Many Horses Were Killed In A Storm" and 1955, "the Winter that Jake Black Bear Froze to Death."

Bits of history float down the river of time until there is no one left to remember, and then they flow into a sea of oblivion. There is no way to quantify Jake Black Bear's frozen mask, the grotesque angles of his pain. He was a man and now he is no more. He was not frozen by the clock's ticking but by the cold.

The Lakota word for *clock* is *mazaskaNskaN* or "moving iron." It stands for a gadget that is not highly respected among Indians. I feel certain that the Indian who first coined that descriptive phrase meant it as a kind of inside joke. Perhaps he even laughed aloud at the white man's pride and downright foolishness in inventing a vacant, numbered face with thin, nervous hands and a stuttering of sound—all to measure something that runs through the fingers like water. Certainly the invention must have struck him as a dramatic example of the white man's penchant for restricting his own freedom and enslaving himself to an abstract concept.

I noticed that not many Indians carried watches and gained the impression that the reason went beyond their inability to afford them. They probably figured it would be like carrying a nagging wife around in your pocket or strapped to your wrist to remind you of a hundred things you didn't really want to be reminded of. Bad-mouthing was always bad, whether done by a screaming wife or an infernal ticking machine, a piece of moving iron.

The Sioux have a word which serves as an antidote to clock time—*toksa* (pronounced *doak-sha*) and it means "until," "by and by," and "I'll do it but in my own good time." It is a word that rolls easily off the tongue, with no hurry about getting out. People are said to be *toksa*, which is a tolerant epithet when used by Indians and carries no stigma. Situations are *toksa*. I remember a hand-printed cardboard sign in a Trading Post window:

Championship softball game tonight!
Starts somewhere around sundown.

Toksa is also a word used in parting as it is the first word in the Sioux expression. *Toksa ake waNciNyaNkiN kte*, "until again I will see you" or "goodbye."

In short, *toksa* stands for a way of life, a life-style—easy, tolerant, and admirably suited to the territory. For children burning the slow, green fuse of summer, *toksa* is the wind-blessed promise of plenty. For the old, who have nothing to do but soak up the summer sun and watch the prairie basins fill up with West, *toksa* is all they need to know of time. For those who remember, *toksa* is a balm. For those who would forget, *toksa* is a salve that heals most wounds. It is a defense against a thousand madnesses perpetrated by speed and alienation, a momentary stay against confusion.

Yet *toksa*, to the uninitiated or the unsympathetic is a word that sums up all the apparent inefficiency and indif-ference to white standards of reservation life. And to these people, *toksa* is an adjective of abuse as it snaps off their tongues like the cracking of a bull whip. The Indian dancing scheduled for six o'clock that doesn't start until after eight is *toksa*. The man who fails to keep an appointment is *toksa*. The low gear, daily routine of reservation life is *toksa*.

To be *toksa* requires a space big enough to get lost in as well as a point of view. A visible horizon. A night full of stars. A river. For *time* and *space* are cousins. City dwellers are *toksa sni*, not *toksa*. The neon world is always young, bubbling through transparent veins. When the bulb burns out it is replaced. When the cathedral lists under its glory-weight it is torn down. The city is always complete with interchangeable parts. The derelict who froze to death in a midnight alley rises with the morning, a Phoenix from the ash of snow. And there is no Winter Count to remember his name. The crowd that flows underground at one corner comes up again at the next. Almost overnight landmarks dissolve. There is only one point of reference—the crystal, eternal *now*. In the city, the *toksa* are the damned.

Today, the concept of Indian-time is a gift as precious as Indian corn once was. And just as life-giving. A concept whose significance goes far beyond that mild antidote, *toska*, which may indeed serve to relieve the quiet desperation of our lives. But there is also the hunger of the spirit.

For now we see through a glass, darkly...

We see time as a point on a linear continuum and proceed to regulate our lives and our affairs according to this restricted angle of vision. There is little sense of continuity with the past, little sense of where-we-have-been. Often we dismiss The Past, as one of our modern poets did, calling it "…a bucket of ashes." Time is something to be endured, exploited, killed or equated with money. Such prevalent attitudes reveal that we glimpse the metaphoric river from a densely-wooded spot on the bank: we don't know its source or its final destination.

But for centuries the American Indian has spoken to us of time and the river. And the Earth it flows through. He *still* speaks to us. His voice is soft yet as persistent as the wind in mountain pines. For the Indian's roots run deep in this native soil. He tells us that time is a part of his sacred web of life, a web that binds man, nature and eternity in a deathless relationship. He speaks of a nearly-forgotten yesterday when men *experienced* more than they *knew*. He warns us of a tomorrow of reckoning if we continue to ignore these sacred bonds. In his cosmic view he offers us the ultimate in second chances—to go home again and to see, not darkly, but face to face.

M A S S   H E R E,

MASS THERE

BEFORE I WENT TO THE Rosebud Sioux Reservation in south-central South Dakota, my Catholicism had been middle class.

That is, rational, affluent, organized, and convenient.

My home parish of St. Thomas was located in the fashionable suburbs. Its congregation was highly educated and so was its clergy. Its buildings, a new church, a rectory, and an elementary school, rose like golden islands in a sea of well-manicured grass. The church was cool in the summer and warm in the winter.

Most of the Gothic interior was done in shining white marble. There was an elaborate sound system that caught even a whisper in its bellows and shivered it around the church until it finally died on an electronic hush. There was an organ that trembled the silence and bells that chimed gentler tunes. The pews were comfortable and the kneeling benches were padded. Even the stained-glass saints that paraded the walls seemed to wear a richer sun in their robes of glory.

I do not mean to imply that there was anything unchristian about such dignified opulence. None of its splendor was rendered to Caesar. All of it was rendered to God. But it was a dramatic contrast to what I experienced while worshiping among the Sioux.

In the summer, the church bells of the tiny reservation community shatter the silence. Before 10 a.m., when the bells first sound for the 10:30 Mass, the June day seems suspended on a breath. The dusty, unpaved streets are like the furrows of a deserted farm. Even the constant, prairie wind seems but a whisper, nudging a stick-ball of tumbleweed down the empty street.

The bells are nagging. There is no escape from their solemn summons.

A half mile from the church, the door of a tar-paper

37

shack opens slowly and a black-shawled old woman steps on skinny legs into the dust. Beaded sneakers stick out from under the hem of her ankle-length dress. In one hand she carries a black umbrella to be used against the noon sun on her return. In the other hand she carries a worn prayer book written in the Lakota language and a knobby, black wooden string of beads dangling a crucifix. The old woman's face is the color of polished mahogany.

As she shuffles painfully down the street toward the ringing of the bells, her shoes kick up tiny explosions of dust behind her. She feels the sun on her face but she does not raise her eyes. The cataracts growing there have cruelly limited her vision to the length of her own shadow in the dust.

A man catches up to her. He wears a blue denim work shirt, blue denim jeans, and a black western hat sprouting an eagle's feather. His dark eyes look out sadly from beneath its wide brim.

The man too is old, older than the woman who is his wife. He has the same mahogany-colored skin, the same well-deep eyes, the same timeless dignity—almost the dignity of a mountain sculptured by the centuries.

Others have started to appear in the street. A middle-aged couple, each holding the hand of a young child, follows the bells. The children dance beside them, their dark button eyes shining with a Sunday excitement.

Old Frank Horn Bear hobbles down the street, already having walked the four long miles from his isolated prairie shack near Grass Mountain. Last night he was a native priest invoking the spirits of the bear, the hawk, and the deer in his attempts to prophesy and cure.

But today he has left the darker world of the spirits and leans on a heavy stick to help him find God. His simple faith is beyond paradox.

In front of the church there is a scattering of battered, dusty cars and pickup trucks. Most of them are ten to twelve years old and rattle along in various stages of disrepair. Wooden racks on the roofs hold the few bald spare tires that make the difference between riding and walking. A few of the cars are new and shiny, bearing the colors of faraway places on their license plates. New York, Vermont, California.

The church is an old, plain wooden building, wearing a new coat of white paint. Its architecture is Prairie Gothic. It has the stark innocence of a little girl in her First Communion dress.

The people, twenty or so, climb the worn, creaking steps. Inside, the church is equally plain. The Stations tell their story around the bare walls. The pews, stiff and formal, wait before a flickering of candles. By the side of the altar, St. Joseph holds a T-square in one hand and balances the Christ Child in the other. There is the ghost of a smile on his face. He seems to approve of the crude carpentry of the dedicated Indians who built the church. "It is finer than halls of marble," his smile assures them, "because you built it with your own hands."

The altar is covered with buffalo hides sewn together. The words: *WakaN, WakaN, WakaN* (Holy, Holy, Holy) are printed in brilliant yellow across the front. The candles are set in buffalo horns.

Behind the altar hangs a huge crucifix. The Christ crucified is an Indian Christ. His long hair is braided; the eyes are dark almonds; the cheekbones are high and shine a gun-metal blue.

Beneath the crucifix is a peace pipe suspended from leather thongs. On one side wall is a painting of a huge thunderbird and, on the opposite wall, a conical tipi covered with a sharp geometry of designs.

The Indian lay reader enters, and the congregation rises to a chorus of squeaks from the wooden benches. Then the priest appears, flanked by two Indian altar boys. The priest wears beaded vestments, a gift from the people of the community. He wears them proudly, knowing that stiff fingers worked many long winter nights sorting the tiny beads.

The chorus begins the first hymn, "Nearer, my God, to Thee," sung in the Lakota language.

Looking around at the people, one is impressed with their poverty, their faith, and their dignity. The people who are assembled here are the poorest of the poor. Most of them have missed meals or filled empty stomachs with heavy starches—Indian fry bread washed down with coffee. The hands of both men and women are rough and calloused; the fingers are spade-shaped. The faces are the faces of the people who have suffered and who wear the marks of their suffering proudly, as a soldier wears his medals. A dark flame still burns like a jet in their eyes no matter how creased and leathery the skin. There is the smoldering triumph of having endured in those eyes.

The children are as restless as all children, anxious to be off and running knee-deep in June. Their dark eyes flash impatience.

The homily is short, but not sweet. It deals in hard,

realistic prose with the evils of alcohol, perhaps the severest social problem on the reservation. The priest talks of broken dreams and broken lives. He cites a member of his congregation who has mended his life by swearing off. He talks of others who drank themselves into early graves. He talks of families abandoned. Of cattle dead of thirst because no one checked the windmills that pumped them water. Of crops unharvested. Of men in jail for crimes committed while in a drunken stupor. Of twisted bodies pulled from the wreckage of automobiles.

His staccato address is punctuated with the guttural, assenting *haus* (yes) and *hecehus* (it is so) of the males in the congregation. The priest concludes his brief sermon in a passionate burst of Lakota: *YatkaN sni yo!* Drink not!

The few tourists present are surprised. There has been no mention of God in the homily. No attempt to relate the Sunday Gospel to the lives of the people. No instruction in matters liturgical. Just an old priest's tirade against liquor.

But the words were not addressed to tourists. The Indians approve. There is not one among them whose life has not been touched by the curse of drink.

When the collection is taken, the men squirm to get their hands into the tight pockets of their jeans and the women open their small, worn purses to select one of their precious coins. The ringing of silver on wicker is the only sound for a few minutes as the basket is passed from hand to hand. One of the tourists puts a bill in the basket. No one turns to look. It would be poor manners to notice, and the Indians would not want to embarrass their guests.

Later in the Mass the priest says: "Let us now offer

39

each other the Sign of Peace." The congregation is small enough so that he can leave the altar to shake the hand of everyone present. The Indian people turn shyly to one another, despite the fact that they meet every day. But the familiar ritual is sanctified by the occasion and the presence of the Lord. A tourist is offered a hard hand bound in raised purple veins. The children shake the hands of other children with exaggerated enthusiasm. A little girl's ring comes off during the handshake. She dives to the floor to find it, her starched white dress sticking up like a bobbing duck's tail feathers.

The priest speaks to the individual members of his parish as he shakes each hand.

"Peace be to you, Ed. How's Sarah?"

"Peace be to you, Howard. Did you find that palomino yet?"

"Peace be to you, Nancy. I've got a tourist who's looking for a beaded purse."

"Peace be to you, Al. I hear Howard's having trouble."

At communion time, every Indian of age rises and heads for the altar. The children start to stampede until firm hands tighten on their shoulders. Then they fall back into their family groups to form a dignified procession.

The priest waits for them before the altar rail. As he places the communion wafer deftly on each tongue, he says: "Body of Christ, Al." "Body of Christ, Nancy." "Body of Christ, Margaret."

When the Mass is over, the people wait for their priest to walk down the aisle and out the front door. They sing a recessional hymn. Then the people file out, stopping to

shake hands with their pastor again on the steps of the church. They mill about on the steps and in the dusty street, talking church business or family business—or just talking.

The sun has climbed higher in the cloudless sky and pours down like molten gold. A few umbrellas are raised, dark mushrooms under which to hide.

For about half an hour the people stand around and visit while the children play noisily. The pastor, still wearing his beaded vestments and now a cowboy hat to protect him from the sun, moves among them, shaking hands ritualistically. Then, when the conversations sputter and die, almost as though on a signal, the people turn and walk their separate ways in he dust.

Just as the prairie brought a new dimension to my concept of space, so the Indian Mass brought a new dimension to my Catholicism. For as men are shaped *by* God, so they seek to shape *Him* to their personal or collective needs. Their Christ of the prairies is an Indian Christ, a man of sorrows with a feather in his hair and the pipe of peace in his hands. A Christ who might suddenly appear on the wings of the thunderbird, as well as on the wings of the dove.

The Christ of the prairies is a waiting Christ, patient as the mountains. A Christ who lives intimately with wind, sand, and stars, and the immense solitude of open places. A Christ in patched jeans moving among the poor, the lonely, and the forgotten, breathing into them the breath of hope.

In the total scheme of things, this Sunday morning on a South Dakota Indian reservation may not account for much. Perhaps no more than a grain of sand on the prairie waste. Six white tourists and twenty-two Indians had spent an hour with God. Most of them were poor people, but they left the inheritors of Christ through his sacraments. Most were lonely, but they left with friends. They had touched Christ and their neighbors' hands. Most were quiet people, but they had given their voices in prayer and song.

And the last two lines of one of their hymns seemed to echo:

Hope gently leading me
Nearer, my God, to Thee.

"WITHOUT MEMORIES"

WE ARE AS THE WIND"

IT HAPPENED ALMOST TWENTY YEARS AGO, ON A HOT JULY day, but I still remember it clearly. The old Indian woman was wearing tennis shoes, an ankle-length dress, and a black shawl. She was carrying an open umbrella for protection against the fierce Dakota sun.

I stopped the car and asked her where she was going.

To a small cemetery five miles west, she told me, on the edge of the Badlands. It was a long walk for a woman I guessed to be in her eighties, especially with the noonday sun beating down on the treeless prairie.

It turned out to be a half hour's drive. The gravel road stopped suddenly, continuing as two tracks across the open prairie. There were washouts, ruts, and bumps that slowed us to a crawl. But time is not so important on the plains. And the minutes were filled by an old woman's remembering.

She was going to visit her son's grave—to sing a song of remembrance and put a few sacred stones in the dust. He had been killed in the war, on some lonely Pacific island back in 1944, only eighteen when he died. She remembered the boy but had never known the man, and so her stories were seen through the eyes of her heart.

She told of his birth in the Moon of Falling Leaves, the white man's November. She told of the time he had wandered off at the Sun Dance at Pine Ridge and was lost for two hours; his first day at school after he had run from the school bus and hidden in the grass; his First Communion; a rattlesnake near the woodpile;

I told her it was a long time to remember, to "throw the mind back," as the Sioux expressed it. I had lost friends in that war, had even seen them die, but now the sorrow had passed and there was only an absence, a kind of negative pain.

"We *must* throw the mind back," she insisted

43

patiently. "Without memories we are as wind in the buffalo grass."

On two occasions I have spoken her words aloud, once in anger and once in reverence.

THE CEMETERY was four dusty graves facing west. Two were unmarked, but my companion told me who was buried in them. One had died in the First World War, a soldier. The other was a child who had died of the measles in the early 1930s. Another gray, weathered stone carried the name of Elijah Jumping Elk and the dates 1900-1954. The fourth grave was her son's.

I stood awkwardly nearby as she reached in a pocket and withdrew two stones, kneeling to place them on the grave. I noticed there was a pile of them now, dropped over the years like solid tears. I knew that flowers would have wilted in an hour, and plastic substitutes weren't a part of her world.

Then she sang in Lakota a simple, trembling chant repeated over and over again:

I remember Billy Two Hawk.
He was a warrior
With a strong heart.
A son,
I remember him.

That was all. That was all that needed to be said. The Great Spirit would know the rest. She made the Sign of the Cross and rose to her feet. I took her home.

By the time I returned to the reservation two years later, she lay beside her son. I put a few stones on her grave—belated payment for some words she had given me

one day, words that have become a part of my own silent requiems for nearly twenty years now.

THE ANGRY WORDS were spoken to an overzealous salesman trying to sell me a word processor. I agreed with him that, in a certain sense, machines have a memory, that data can be stored and recalled later at the touch of a button. But in talking about what he called Random Access Memory, he concluded his pitch, "It has a memory like a mother's."

Instantly my own memory system was activated: an old Indian woman was dropping stones and prayers on a lonely grave near the Dakota Badlands. She was stooped and her leathery face was webbed with the lines of living. She didn't look much like the young woman operating the machine in the salesman's brochure. And the old woman's memory wasn't "Random Access." It was painfully selective.

A memory like a mother's?

"Not hardly," I told him. "More like wind in the buffalo grass."

I never bought the word processor, perhaps because memory is more sacred to me than it was twenty years ago. Perhaps because I feel memory should be accompanied by laughter or tears or some human feeling. It wasn't the salesman's fault. He was just doing his job. But in boasting of a machine's memory he had unknowingly tread on mine.

44

THE OTHER TIME I said her words aloud was at an all Souls' Day Mass.

During the homily my mind wandered. I was thinking of this holy day that the Church has set aside for remembrance. And then in my mind the long parade of the dead began filing past, the faces that matched the list of names on the envelope I had put in the collection basket a week earlier. The parade started with a classmate in first grade and came up through the recent death of a good friend. Maybe fifty years of remembering.

And then it came to me that the Church had elevated memory to a sacramental rite. The Mass itself was the celebration of a living memory. And there was the calendar: almost every day of the year was devoted to the memory of some saint. The collective memory of the Catholic Church stretches back 2,000 years.

And it was then that I said it: "Without memories we are as wind in the buffalo grass." A few heads turned, but it was worth it to me—hearing her words spoken aloud again.

Growing older means living more intimately with memories. The eternal present may be good enough for youth, but maturity demands more of us. Memories give a continuity, a sense of purpose to our lives. They echo back across the years those voices and images from the past telling us what we are and, if we are very lucky, what we should become.

P H O T O G A L L E R Y

TWO

Sherry Makes Room for Them giving Rocky a bath

Corrine Cloudman's "Transitional" house

Victor Makes Room for Them painting

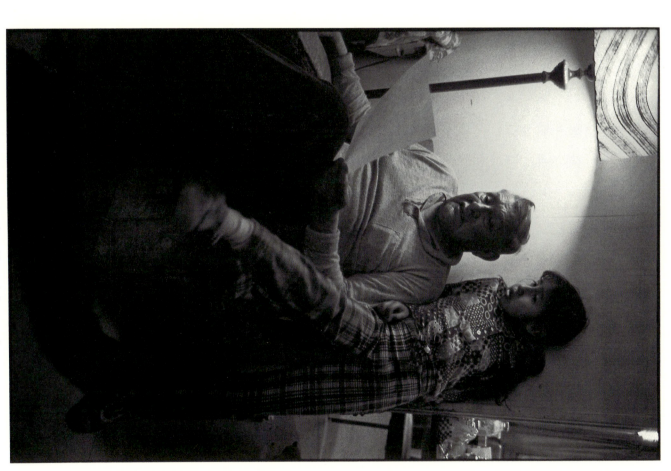

Noah Kills in Sight reviews his grandaughter Eleanor's homework

Nellie Redbird and Daniel White Hat

Eleanor Kills in Sight in her first communion dress

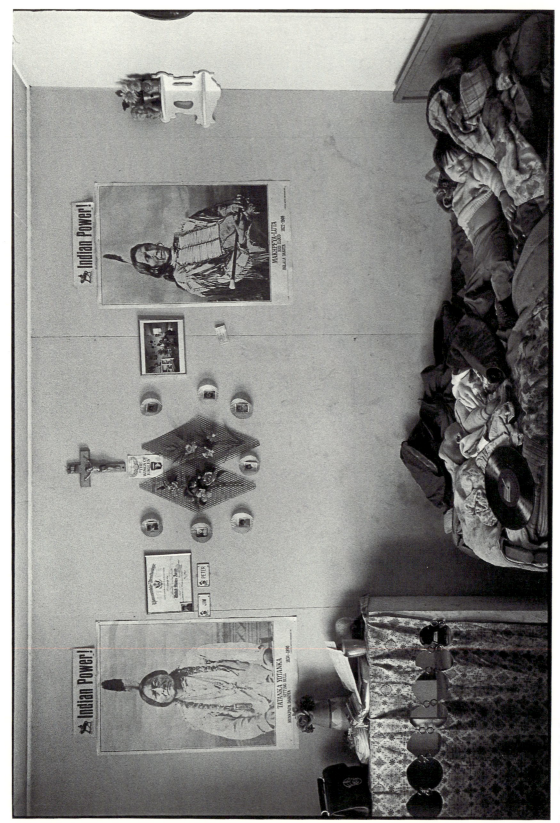

Peter Swift Hawk's home

Orville and Ophelia Kills in Sight with Junior

Victor Makes Room for Them hunting deer

Gordon Swift Hawk

Saturday afternoon: Kenny Kills in Sight, Wendell White Eyes, "Yogi Bear" Left Hand Bull, Rafael Kills in Sight, and Brian Left Hand Bull

Morris Kills in Sight, Glenford Walking Eagle, Ambrose, Sylvan and Daniel White Hat

Graduation at St. Francis Indian School

David Kills in Water

Team and Wagon leading Harvey Walking Eagle's funeral procession

THE LAST CHRISTIAN

I WAS ON SOUTH DAKOTA'S PINE RIDGE SIOUX RESERVATION, and I had been visiting an old Indian. He was a Truth Keeper and knew many of the old myths, legends, and songs that I was collecting that summer.

He was in his nineties, and blind; indeed, the old man was dying. But he wouldn't go the Public Health Service Hospital; he wanted to die at home. So his seventy-year-old son and his middle-aged grandchildren had been bringing him groceries and water during his long, self-imposed exile.

He had given me directions on how to reach the paved head terri-

highway, but the map inside his head bore little resemblance to the territory.

"road" he remembered turned out to be two wagon ruts separated by

a high center, a trail washed out by spring rains and baked to a cracked web by the summer sun.

"Turn east at the trading post," he had told me. But there was no trading post. I found out later that it had burned to the ground ten years before. "Turn south by the windmill, at Jake Black Bear's place." But there was no windmill, and Jake Black Bear's place had long since been devoured by the wild hunger of prairie grass.

Soon I was lost, but I continued following the ruts, heading east across the open prairie, thinking that I would intersect the highway before too many miles. In ten minutes I knew I was right, for the sharp peak of Eagle Butte rose from the ground swell like a beacon, reflecting in pastels the late afternoon sun. It was a welcome reference point in a country of few landmarks.

THEN AS I CAME OVER the crest of a knoll, I suddenly noticed an abandoned church, several hundred yards from the road. It was a plain wooden structure, weathering gray against the blue Dakota sky. As I approached it, the church seemed to sail backward in a prairie sea, a derelict hulk that somehow had not sunk beneath the waves of grass.

I don't know why I stopped. Perhaps from sheer surprise—the kind of surprise you feel when you see a window light in a house you thought was empty. Or from an Easterner's affinity for the vertical in a land of horizontals. Or, perhaps, from some secret, hurting fear that He, too, might have deserted a place that Indian believers once called holy.

Whatever the reason, I stopped and climbed the gentle hill from which the church kept its lonely vigil over the empty miles.

Looking about, I wondered what community the church might have served. Nothing rose above the prairie tide for miles, except Eagle Butte and some cottonwoods, waiting in silver rows on dry creek banks for the sudden swell of rain. The vestiges of any communal life—tarpaper shacks, rusting car bodies, windmills to pump water from the flinty soil, or even barbed wire tuned to a prairie wind—were nowhere to be seen.

But even as a stranger, I knew that man's homely monuments did not last long in this timeless land. Out here, the elements conspired against upward-thrusting things; in time, only the dream reached high. Here the Earth's pulse beat heavily, shaking man loose from any permanence. Yet the church stood there, as though carved from the land, almost a faith unto itself.

As I stepped up and over the three rotting steps, I saw a cardboard sign tacked to the door. Its words were faded and barely legible. *No Trespassing*, it warned, and bore the heavy signature: *Tribal Police.* But a rusted padlock had been broken, and the door, opening and closing gently in the wind, dared me to enter.

It is difficult to pass them by—mine shafts, graveyards, ghost towns—those deserted places where the clues to our own mortality lie scattered about. Places where the past hangs like a heavy tapestry in the chambers of the heart. Most of us are amateur archaeologists, sifting dust or sand for the connections that hurt. The arrowhead. The broken spinning wheel. The china doll's head. The human bone. All are fragments of spent lives that touch ours, speaking to us with the awkward heart-stuttering of broken and abandoned things.

I stepped over the hasty altar and entered the church. *Forgive us our trespasses.* Inside, the darkness of boarded windows was sliced by the sunlight that poured through the cracks. A single stained glass window remained, its lower half shattered as though by an explosion. But the martyred Mohawk nun, Kateri Tekakwitha, rose above the ruins. Beneath her crudely lettered name, a cross-weary Christ fell for the second time. And above the altar there was a pale and faded emptiness where He had found his dying place.

On either side of the altar there were pastels of Thunderbirds and crossed peace pipes, and the Lakota words *WakaN, WakaN, WakaN*—Holy, Holy, Holy.

A SINGLE OVERTURNED wooden box sat in the center of the floor, as though inviting the intruder to celebrate a holy absence. And a painted angel, frozen in heavy flight above the altar, pointed a chubby finger at where the tabernacle should be. *Why seek ye the living among the dead? Behold the place where they laid Him!*

I crossed the squeaking floor and sat down, looking no doubt like the stunned survivor of a bombed and gutted building. The feeling that came over me was arctic in its pain—the feeling that I was the last, the very last, to know this place for what it once was. That I was the last Christian, as someone must be sometime, if only because the Lord promised an ending.

As I sat there, hunched over my thoughts, the pillars of the day seemed to buckle and the sky to come crashing down. I had the feeling that, after 2000 years, the Christian experience threatened to end, here, in this unlikely spot where neglect was a way of life. Other endings appealed more to the imagination. The tolling of solemn bells. The hymning of an angelic host. Earthquake. Darkness at noon. A voice from the mountaintop. A warning spelled out in the stars. Signs worthy of the final drama. Not the smokeless fires of decay slowly consuming a deserted church on the American prairie.

Then I remembered the *beginning*—how it all took place in a manger, while the rest of the world went on as though nothing had happened. If it all began in a stable in Bethlehem, why couldn't it end here in this abandoned church?

So it had all come down to this moment. The long history. The triumph and the tragedy. All of the drama, faith, sacrifice, and endurance. It all ended here, not in tongues of fire, but in the whispers of prairie wind, before an abandoned altar, a broken saint, and a middle-aged collector of songs.

THEN, QUITE SUDDENLY, it was over, as though the curtain had fallen on the last act. The spell was broken; the illusion gone. Everything was as it seemed. I looked at my watch, following the second hand as it swept a minute into my past. A sound like clumsy applause turned me around, but it was only the door slamming in the wind. I looked at my watch again: 5:30. Time to be going. I think I sighed my relief as I rose awkwardly from the wooden box. I was an unlikely keeper of the keys of any kingdom.

Yet a few questions persisted. What if it had been true? What if it really had ended here? What if I were the last believer?

The questions followed me to the door, diving on my imagination like angry swallows. And like a hungry beggar my mind searched the years, scavenging for the fragments of my faith. A parade of Latin phrases, solemn as robed monks. A dozen Gospels, star-lit by Luke's Nativity. A sorting of beads into prayer. Five or six hymns. Snatches of a liturgy from a Sunday Missal. The Stations of the Cross in a confused ordering of sorrow. Ten or twelve prayers, a spiritual bequest from my grandmother, although only one was used in the Mass now. A choir of stained glass saints. A memory of dark corners trembling with organ music. A clasping of hands. The stirring of a soul.

These fragments were all I had. Not enough to reconstruct a faith. Little history, doctrine, or liturgy. Just a *feeling* for a living God, a fragile legacy for those who would follow, perhaps thirsting for belief.

I STEPPED OUT into the sunlight, blinking from the glare and some lingering doubts. In a few minutes the light had penetrated the dark corners; I was once again caught up in the present. The mind can take only so much inner wandering; then, like the needle of a compass, it swings back to the compelling force outside. Maybe that is why so few of us are saints: the outer realities prove to be the strongest.

As I stood there and gazed west, I noticed a fenced-in area behind the church, a graveyard, knee-deep in neglect. The rusted iron fence rose and fell like a graph, and the bleached, porous headstones seemed as some sparse and random harvest of memory. A faded and shredded American flag scored the wind. Several red-tipped prayer-sticks, their turkey feathers still turning, stirred forgetfulness. A few colored stones lay on the graves like frozen tears, afraid to melt. Some scattered plastic flowers looked sadder, perhaps, because they refused to wilt.

Most of the names on the headstones had been worn away. But a few names were still visible, the ghost of someone's labor, someone's love. Martha Yellow Cloud, 1825-1912. Ruben Charging Thunder, dates eroded. Noah Kills the Enemy. Rest in Peace. Beloved son…

Half surprising myself, I dropped to one knee and said an Our Father over the smoldering fuse to eternity that was Ruben Charging Thunder. I mixed two Hail Marys with the dust of Martha Yellow Cloud. And I straightened the flag over Noah Kills the Enemy.

I struggled to pick up one fallen headstone, and when I had set it upright again the name leaped out at me: Henry Good. On the bare spot where the marker had depressed the prairie soil there was a delicate sprinkling of Indian beads, brought up from the grave by ants in some piecemeal ritual of resurrection.

I don't know why I said those prayers, straightened the flag, or raised the headstone. Perhaps even the dead can cry out for attention. But I was still on one knee when the question struck again, like lightning from a cloudless sky. *What if you were the last believer?* And before I could think of an answer or dismiss the question, a story from my boyhood rose in my mind like something suddenly released from the bottom of a muddy pond.

It was a story about St. Francis. He was hoeing his garden one day when a friend interrupted his labors to talk. The friend asked, "What would you do if you knew that the world would end tomorrow?" St. Francis replied, "I would finish hoeing my garden."

Whether the story is apocryphal, or which St. Francis is credited with the words, I do not know. But they had answered the question that had followed me from deserted church to graveyard: *What if you were the last believer?*

I would do what I had done. I would finish what I had started. I would say a prayer or two for the long dead and perhaps a few more for the soon to die. I would straighten a flag, raise a headstone, and perhaps re-tie a turkey feather on a prayerstick. I would say the name of Ruben Charging Thunder aloud, pronouncing his immortality to an indifferent wind. I would retrieve some plastic flowers from the corner of an abandoned church, and set them on the dust of Martha Yellow Cloud. And then I would watch the sun set, wondering where in eternity East might be.

NOAH JUMPING EAGLE

IT WAS LATE IN THE SUMMER OF '64, THE SKY OVER THE Dakota prairie was cloudless and a hurting blue.

Noah Jumping Eagle walked ahead of me leading the way toward the banks of the Little White River, which meanders darkly through the Rosebud Sioux Reservation, adding still another age-line to the face of the land.

Noah was a big man who had started to settle beneath the weight of his years. He had a classic Indian face with sharp, chiseled features and dark, liquid eyes.

In most places I can think of, Noah would have been considered slightly mad or, at the very least, wildly eccentric. But here, in this mystical land among a mystical people, many considered him a holy man. He was as respected as a priest or surgeon might have been in another community. Mystics go with the territory.

Noah Jumping Eagle was a practicing Catholic, a pillar of his tiny parish in the Spring Creek community, but he was also an Indian and his imagination leaped to where the air was thinner and the more orthodox feared

to follow. He tracked his God like a hunter—through the rimrocked canyons, over eroded, tabletop buttes, and even across the star trail.

He hungered after God—not just the *idea* of God, but the living flesh. And finally in his sixty-seventh year, he found God.

I believed him. I had known he was a man of faith ever since the day we were discussing the drought in the East, one of the worst in years. Water supplies were dangerously low, and the governor had declared a state of emergency. When our conversation had trailed off into a solemn shaking of heads, Noah startled me with his simple proposal.

"Why don't you use prayer?"

"Some of us probably do pray," I answered vaguely. "Farmers and people like that."

He shook his head. "I mean *together*," he said, as though he were speaking to a child who didn't quite understand. "A state day of prayer. When everybody prays together. So God will be sure to hear."

Suddenly I thought I knew how Peter felt when the cock crowed for the third time. How Thomas felt when his finger found the nail holes. I, too, was one of little faith.

As an outsider, an Easterner, and an academic doing research on the legends of the Sioux, I was a prisoner of the culture that had shaped me. I saw through St. Paul's glass darkly and might never come to see face to face.

It was a sad, even a frightening thought. Noah and I shared the same God, yet he was free to run the hounds of heaven while I must wait, sifting the heart's evidence against the head's.

"It is not far now," Noah said, breaking into my thoughts, grinning his gold-toothed grin.

After another five minutes, Noah turned back to me. "The holy tree," he said softly in Lakota, the language of the trans-Missouri Sioux.

I saw it. The holy tree. A huge cottonwood rising like a fountain. This was the tree, according to Noah Jumping Eagle, in which a vision of the Lord had appeared to him—not once, but every Friday throughout the summer.

Noah pointed to a V made by the meeting of the two largest branches on the tree. "There," he said pointing. "There is where He stands."

A shiver of expectation ran through me. At the same time, I remembered the words of a priest friend when I had told him about Noah's invitation to visit the holy tree.

"You won't see anything," he told me matter-of-factly. And then added, somewhat sadly I recalled, "Only those who have already found God can see Him like that." I didn't know what he meant then. I do now.

My friend had been a missionary to the Sioux for twelve years and had never ceased to wonder at their faith. It almost seemed as though he were jealous of their mystical ties with the land and the Great Spirit, who was also the Christ.

But the heightened sense of anticipation would not leave. And so we stood, looking up into the rustling cottonwood. I looked at my friend. In profile, with the sun pouring over his features, he looked like a hawk on fire. A predatory God-seeker.

Suddenly he slumped to his knees, bent his head, and struck his breast three times.

"My Lord and my God!" The words broke from him like a sob, and I found myself kneeling beside him in the dust. As I knelt, I raised my eyes to the tree, searching the V of its branches. I saw nothing. Nothing but the upturning of silver leaves. In the back of my mind I kept hearing the echo of my priest friend's sad prediction: "Only those who have already found God can see Him like that."

Then, without any warning, Noah broke into song, "Great Spirit, have pity on me!"

He sang it four times and then four times four in a tuneless chant that was almost a keening. His body shook. Then his voice faded and there were only the prairie sounds—the wind shaking the tree, the gurgling of the river, and the drone of locusts sawing on the afternoon.

After half an hour or so, Noah rose and without speaking a word, started back toward the tar-paper shack that he called home.

Later that night, in the flickering light of a kerosene lamp, Noah and I drank coffee. He was still visibly shaken from the effects of his visit to the holy tree. His gnarled fingers trembled around the warmth of the tin cup as a novice priest's might have trembled on the chalice. He had not spoken for hours, since the song had burst from him. Now he was returning to the everyday world, a dream at a time.

"I didn't see anything," I said, my words falling awkwardly, I felt as though I were making my confession to an indifferent priest.

He continued to sip his coffee, holding the cup with both hands. He reminded me of a Second World War photograph I had seen. A merchant seaman whose ship had been torpedoed from under him was clutching a mug of coffee. A blanket covered all but the dazed expression on his face.

"I saw nothing," I repeated.

Noah nodded, his face expressionless. Then the tight seam of his mouth moved like the opening and closing of a leather purse. "But He saw you."

That was all he ever said. When I left his cabin later that night, it was for the last time. The following summer when I returned, I learned that my friend had died during the winter. He had frozen to death. Somewhere by the holy tree.

I tried to find out where he was buried, but none of the Indians would talk about Noah. I checked the tribal offices, and they had no details. Finally, I went to see my friend at the mission.

"Noah was a good Catholic," he told me. "He's in holy ground."

The next morning I went alone to the holy tree. It was a jewel of a day, very like the one on which Noah and I had made our visit together. As I came within sight of the river, the feeling came over me that I had traveled in a giant circle and had returned to my point of departure. Memories drifted like lazy clouds across the span of time.

The tree seemed smaller somehow, as though I were seeing it through the wrong end of a telescope. I felt like a man returned to the scenes of his childhood who finds things dwarfed by absence.

I went to the far side of the tree. There was a mild depression in the earth there, a settling that I recognized. A chunk of rough jade as big as a man's fist and a withered branch from the holy tree were stuck in the ground. A prayer stick, its top painted red and dangling a turkey feather, leaned over at an odd angle.

I looked around, trying to imagine what the tranquil place was like with the winter wind lashing the kneeling tree. I tried to imagine what might happen to a man who fell through the ice and froze his legs. I tried; but the distance was too great. I was only a summer friend.

I felt that I should say something over the place. But there was nothing to say. Noah had said it all when he knelt before the holy tree, borrowing the words of an anguished Thomas. I made the Sign of the Cross, the sign language for what I felt inside.

A D E A T H

ON THE PRAIRIE

I BECAME A WITNESS TO THE OLD INDIAN'S DEATH QUITE BY accident. I was doing research for a book on the songs of the Sioux, and my work led me to his prairie shack on the edge of the Badlands in South Dakota. One of my informants in Pine Ridge Town had told me about old Elijah, how he knew hundreds of songs, some going back to prereservation times. That was all the encouragement I needed, so I bought several bags of groceries and some tobacco, and loading my tape recorder and camera into my station wagon I set out, following the twin ruts that led west across the stubbled prairie grass.

From the beginning it seemed like a journey back in time. As I bounced along, leaving a wake of dust behind me, I watched the unfolding emptiness that swept like a tide toward the horizon. A loneliness translated into place. I passed an abandoned church brooding on a hilltop, waiting for the slow stream of worshipers that would never come again. A few miles later I saw a tar-paper shack that had collapsed upon itself, its own gray and formless

monument to neglect. Overhead a hawk floated across the setting sun in a bloody crucifixion. And beyond, to the north and west, I could see the Badlands coming into focus, scarred and pitted like the surface of the moon.

Makoce Sica, the Sioux called it, that stretch of gray desolation—the Badlands. And yet they found a beauty in that furious erosion: Historically it had been a refuge and a retreat. A place to hide; a place to pray. A white man could only find it curious and frightening, a setting for science fiction. But to some Indians it was a sacred and holy place.

Elijah's home sat on the eastern edge of that ashen emptiness like a guardian, brooding

75

over a geometry of lengthening shadows. His cabin of wood scraps and tar paper seemed as temporary as the Gothic spires beyond seemed permanent. A reminder, perhaps, of the frailty of man's efforts and the endurance of things created by the Great Spirit. Already his weather-beaten cabin listed from the constant wind. Already it had turned death gray and assumed the waiting attitude of prairie things that seemed to float on a sea of time.

Old Elijah was sitting on the careworn steps of his cabin, his creased, mahogany face following the failing sun like a dark blossom. When I drove up in an explosion of dust, he drew himself to his feet wearily, as though he had been interrupted from something important, and hobbled toward me in his worn cowboy boots.

I introduced myself, speaking in Lakota, which pleased him. I had heard he was a good singer, I told him, and knew many of the songs from the faraway times. He nodded and said it was good to hold on to the old things. Soon they would be as the wind in the buffalo grass. I unloaded the groceries, explaining they were a donation for any help he could give me with the songs, especially the old ones that were dying with the people who were old. Soon they would be gone forever, I said, like our yesterdays.

He nodded, a heavy sadness filling his filmy eyes. "It is good you have come today," he said softly. "For tomorrow I must go away."

I didn't pay much attention to his words at the time. I supposed that his relatives or some friends were going to pick him up and take him to Rapid City or maybe to one of the Indian celebrations that filled the weekends during the summer months. I never imagined he was speaking of the big journey to the Spirit Land.

We sat outside on the steps watching the darkness fall. In the west the outline of boiling clouds could be seen and the distant lightning began stitching the earth to the sky. I knew the storm could hit or pass us by completely. That is the way with prairie storms: They follow some capricious compass of their own.

"*Wakinyan*," Elijah said, nodding toward the gathering storm. *Wakinyan*, the Thunderbird, whose eyes flashed lightning and wings flapped thunder. It was a good image, I thought, one that the poetic imagination might easily accept in that mystical place.

In ten minutes or so the fury of the storm was upon us. From inside the cabin we could hear the cascade of rain and the sharp explosions of thunder. The wind ripped at the cabin like something gone mad and drove the rain through the roof in silver splinters. Elijah lit one of the kerosene lamps that hung from the rafters, sat down in a huge chair that was shedding its stuffing, and waited.

As I looked out the only window in the room into the angry face of the storm, a quotation from the Bible, from II Kings, crossed my mind: "…and Elijah went up by a whirlwind into heaven." It was strange, I thought, how ancient words returned to light the moment, even as the lightning turned the pages of night with a fiery finger. Elijah was the prophet who returned as the herald of the Messiah, the one referred to by Jesus in the Transfiguration. I looked at the old man across from me, wondering if he too could be a prophet of his people, the failing repository of their wisdom in legend and song.

I knew that the storm would force me to stay the night: The rains would turn even the ruts I had followed into a sea of mud. But in a way I was glad. I felt that there were things to be learned from this old man, who had lived through so much and who had stored so much of it in his heart.

After the storm passed and the air turned fresh and cool, we ate a simple meal of canned tomatoes, bread and coffee. Then we smoked in silence, a silence that was like a communion as he blew his smoke toward earth, sky, and the four directions to ensure the presence of the Great Spirit. Finally, he spoke in Lakota: "I can see that you have come with a good heart," he said in a frail and trembling voice. "I can see that you want to catch the songs of the people in that box so they will not be lost forever. So that the young people may remember. *Heceetu.* It is so. I will sing for you."

A FEW MINUTES LATER I turned on my battery-operated recorder and his high falsetto began to fill the room. Sometimes he accompanied himself on a small drum he held on his lap. His eyes closed, his head thrown back, he looked like one in a trance as the songs were drawn from memory like healing water from a deep well. Strong heart songs, ceremonial songs, healing songs, dream songs, council songs, honor songs, love songs—they all broke from his husky throat like something alive and imprisoned for a long time. Tears coursed down the furrows in his face as he sang the songs that had been handed down from his parents or grandparents, his loving legacy of dreams. He introduced each song in his own language and I did not interrupt him except to put a new tape into the recorder.

When the session was suddenly over, I had four hours of recordings and an old man's most precious possessions, the songs and prayers that had sustained him and his people. Then he told me about himself—how he had seen more than ninety winters, having been born in the same year that Crazy Horse was killed by the soldiers at Fort Robinson. How, for a brief moment in history, he had as a child known the old, free life. How he had lived through the massacre at Wounded Knee in December of 1890 and survived the terrible memory of his family killed, their bodies frozen in the grotesque sculptures of winter death. How he had seen his people delivered into bondage. How he had seen the old ways neglected, abandoned. How he had seen sacred things ignored and new ways and a new tongue take over. It was a liturgy of sorrow and pain that ended with the words: *Oyasin henala,* everything is gone....

Not quite, I said to myself. Not quite everything is gone, Elijah. There is an old man's dignity and courage. There is an old man's caring. And sharing. There is an old man's faith. Such things do not die any more than the wind dies....

I wish I had said these things to him. It is too late now.

Instead, I asked if I might stay overnight. He made a gesture with an arthritic claw of a hand: My house is your house. I went out, got my sleeping bag and returned. Old Elijah was pouring sand from tin cans onto the earthen floor of the cabin. I watched as he drew some things from a leather medicine bag—bird feathers, sage and sweetgrass, a buffalo skull, some colored bits of cloth, a bone whistle. He was making preparations for a ceremony of some kind. I wondered why he didn't go to bed and get some sleep. I looked at my watch. It was after two in the morning, and he was taking a trip in a matter of hours perhaps. Suddenly he began to chant softly in a heavy sing-song voice, something about the hills and how they endure forever. Listening to the rise and fall of hypnotic rhythms, I fell asleep.

A SLANT OF SUNLIGHT coming in the window awakened me. I looked around for my host but he was gone. Perhaps he had left already on his trip, I thought. In the center of the floor there was an altar of sand with the four directions marked by tin cans containing miniature flags of colored cloth. There were also feathered prayer sticks stuck in small piles of sand. I had witnessed most of the ceremonies of the Sioux, but I couldn't identify the one Elijah had performed, perhaps was still performing. Then I heard the sound of muffled drums from somewhere outside, carried to me on the prairie wind. I followed the sound and it led me behind the cabin to a purification lodge made of willow branches bent in the shape of an inverted bowl and covered with a crazy patchwork of canvas and animal skins. The opening faced east and inside I could see clouds of steam rising from the heated rocks.

Old Elijah was naked except for a breechclout. His skin sagged on his bones and hung in folds like leather

clothing that was too large. The livid scars of countless flesh sacrifices to the sun and the spirits formed a curious design on his chest, upper arms and back. He was seated like a frail Buddha, beating on his drum and singing in a hoarse and croaking voice. This time I could make out the words:

This land is good.
O Sun
now
for the last time
come greet me again.

The old man was singing his death song!

Suddenly I could hear the echo of his words to me: "For tomorrow I must go away." I remembered, too, his solitary, early-morning ceremony with its song about the enduring hills. It had all been a ritualistic preparation for his death and I was the inheritor of his last bequest—the blood truths of his songs. And now his death song was the last he would sing, and it would go unrecorded except in my mind. I listened as he sang it again and again, over the beating of the drum and the wind song in the grass, his passionate song to the world that never sang to him, as pure and lyrical as any sounds of leaving.

The white man in me had questions: Why are you dying? How do you know? Is there anything that can be done? But the Indian in me said simply and softly: Leave him alone. It is a *wakaN*, a sacred time, this leaving of one land for another. Everyone is alone at such a time. You will be, too.

But what about his family and friends? the white man insisted.

He has outlived them. They are of another time, another place. They have gone on ahead; they will be waiting on the star trail.

But how can I leave a dying man? There must be something that can be done.

There is. But only he can do it.

I stood there for a minute, watching, listening. Only once did Elijah look up from his song, and in that instant our eyes met and a truth passed between us, a truth so compelling that I turned immediately and walked back toward the cabin.

The next day, while having lunch at the Crazy Horse Cafe, I heard the first public reference to his passing. The place was crowded and people were talking about it.

"How'd he die?" someone asked.

"They don't know," a white man said. "They got to do an autopsy to find out the reason. Probably jus' old age, though. He must have been pushing a hundred."

"Autopsy won't show anything," an Indian said solemnly.

"Why not?"

"Not with Indians like Elijah. Old people like him die when it's time, that's all. There don't have to be reasons other than their own."

And that was the closest thing to a eulogy I was to hear.

I didn't attend Elijah's funeral or the interment. I had been a witness to the real ending that was also a beginning, and I felt that the public ceremony could add nothing to that singular experience. And it was painful for me to accept the idea that he might be buried in a crowded cemetery. Somehow I hoped he would find his rest on the hilltop at Wounded Knee or perhaps near his bleak and barren home, where the spirits of the place still whispered to the buffalo grass and the wind sang free. A truer requiem for a prairie prophet!

Some days later, there were a few columns about him in the weekly newspaper. A social worker had discovered the body when he had gone out to Elijah's isolated cabin to help him fill out some forms. Much was made of the fact that he was reputed to be the oldest Indian on the reservation at the time of his death and that he had been a survivor of Wounded Knee, the very last. The article said there were no living relatives and concluded with details of the funeral and burial. The facts were all there, but somehow it wasn't the truth. Any more than the autopsy report would be the truth....

Old Elijah had sung me a better version!

O, *WakaNtaNka!* Great Spirit! Christ! Lord!
Truthfully, as the Eagle soared
I send these words to Thee:
Let Thy People be!
Be still a part of winters gone
As *Wi*, the Sun, is part of dawn,
Throwing the mind back across the years
To when the world was dry of tears.
Let the eye of the heart choose to see
The path of the circle eternally:
The travelled way from birth to death,
Far as the star trail, near as breath.
Let the People find their center soon
Before the no-returning Moon
Washes the good dream out to sea.

O, let Thy People be!